How to Plan a

Quinceanera

On any Budget

By J. Hilton Dies

A Newbiz Playbook Publication

ISBN-13: 978-1544245775
FIRST EDITION

For downloadable tools emailed directly to you please email products@newbizplaybook.com use the password quince in the re: of the email

For my family, the answer to my why

How to Use this Book

I wrote this book because of widespread demand from consumers of some of my other work on Wedding and Event Planning. I got special requests from families and Planners who wanted to plan a Quinceanera for a special child, some of whom lacked the proper perspective or familiarity with traditions and customs to provide their clients with the level of service they wanted to achieve.

This book is meant to serve both. Not all chapters will be helpful to all audiences, but this book has been designed to contain everything you might need to successfully plan one of these events.

There are a number of tools contained in these pages, and I am happy to make all of them available to you in electronic form so that you may customize them to meet your personal or business needs.

Much of the information contained here will spill over into other kinds of event planning, including sections on interviewing venues, photographers etc., but the hope is that ultimately you will feel that you received value well in excess of what you paid for this book.

Also, know that if I recommend a website or service, I am not receiving any compensation of any kind from them. It is important to me as an author that there be no ambiguity as to where my loyalty rests. It rests with my reader.

To receive the electronic tools contained herein, please email us at **products@newbizplaybook.com** use the password quince in the re: of the email.

Enjoy!

Understanding Your "Product"

Whether you are doing it for family on a budget, or for hire, the fundamental truth about the Quinceanera is that the product is meant to be a dream that celebrates the traditional passage into adulthood for a beloved daughter. Many of the people looking for your expertise have imagined this moment for their children, from the time they were born. Your task is to deliver that perfect day. One of the biggest mistakes that new planners make is to try to use low prices, or the perception of discounted value to attract customers. If you are planning the event for your own family, you want it to run smoothly and be a joy filled event for friends and family. If you are doing it for hire, your customers don't want the cheap option, and what's more they will be less likely to hire someone offering it.

People who hire professionals for this service are looking for an elite experience, for you that means incredible responsiveness. You provide a cell phone. You answer emails within hours if not minutes. For that your customers will pay a premium. Your image, dress, tone, and interactions create this experience.

Nordstrom's is not an inexpensive store. Their products are expensive, even more expensive than other stores by a fair margin, but their client service and return policies are exceptional. The Ritz Carlton hosts very nice facilities, but honestly for the cost, they are not materially better than many less expensive hotels. The difference is in service, and the way they make their patrons feel.

Ignore this fundamental truth, and none of these contents will matter. Embrace it, and you will succeed. The goal is to create Raving Fans at every opportunity. The clients you help will have friends and family getting married, and you want them to insist on you to handle them.

Cost Projections

One of the first questions you will have or get from those who hire you is how to plan for costs of a Quinceanera.

The following is meant to be a guideline. Keep in mind that if you are planning this event for hire, you may be charging by the hour ($75-$350 per hour is not uncommon), as a percentage of the cost of the event (10-20% is the typical range here), or if you have the venue and are hosting in your own location, you may simply charge a total price. This will impact client costs, and should be taken into consideration.

Custom invitations will range from 1-5 dollars depending on whether they are specially printed, the design used, and the quantity ordered. For those on a budget, custom invitations are available in bulk for as little as 70 cents each. If you choose this option, we recommend that you order examples early to ensure that the product meets your expectations. (see inviteshop.com)

Professional catering ranges from a low of $15 dollars per adult to more than $100 depending upon the food, whether the venue is included, and the number of people. This would not include a high end tiered cake, which will cost between $1-3 dollars per slice. If friends and family are helping to prepare the food, I have seen creative folks get that cost to between $2.50 and $3.00 a person using traditional Spanish and Mexican dishes.

Venue costs can vary widely nationwide, and even in particular areas, depending on peak times. Expect to pay between $500 and $2500 for most venues, and with a larger group that number can get much higher. If the Venue is one that is owned by a friend or family, you can often save a lot of money. If you plan to have your party outside, consider lining up tent rental, as weather can kill your event if you are not careful. Tent rental can range from 1-3 dollars per square foot including installation and delivery, so you may not be saving as much as you think.

Entertainment Costs are as follows:

DJ $500 - $1500 depending upon the amount of time, and whether additional light packages, extra sound equipment (such as karaoke), etc. are requested. DJ's are recommended for most parties as bands may have less ability to entertain the group which is very likely to be quite diverse at these events. Obviously, with the ability to store massive amounts of music on phones and tablets, and with the advent of high quality inexpensive DJ apps, music can be provided at a very low cost. This is harder than it looks. If a friend or family member is going to help here, they should practice, and plan the music playlist, or your event will definitely feel the difference.

If small children are involved, face painters, magicians, and other party hosts that provide party or arcade games usually start in the $400 range and go up depending upon the request. Balloon animals and other forms of entertainment may be also be popular. Some of this can be easily done by friends and family with just a little practice. Simple face painting ideas are easily available online.

Extras

Flowers – These range from simple arrangements that can be obtained for less than $500, to more elaborate decorations that rival the cost of weddings in the $2000-$4000 range.

Gifts for attendees – They can be thoughtful photo packages of the quest of honor, or a simply made photo booth with props, which are less expensive, or t-shirts and more that add up. These are absolutely a function of your preference.

Manicures, Pedicures, Hair and Makeup – Don't ignore these as they will add up during your Quinceanera, though they are fun for daughter, sister, mother, and grandmother to do together.

Very often activities will be planned that also double as gifts for the kids in attendance. Examples of these include, candy making bars, wax hands, design your own flip flops etc.,

Industry estimates show that typical Quinceanera cost between $5,000 and $20,000 dollars, but these numbers are skewed as many families choose to host their own events, and privately subcontract catering etc., which wouldn't involve the "industry," much at all.

We have attached a simple budget tool here, but can send an electronic version upon request to products@newbizplaybook.com

Service or Vendor	Estimated Cost	Actual Cost	Deposit Due	Balance Due
Banquet Hall				
Caterer & Bar				
DJ/Band				
Photography				
Videography				
Decorations				
Invitations/Postage				
Entertainment				
Florist				
Event Planner				
Favors & Gifts				
Clothing				
Cake				
Personal Expenses				
Rental Items				
Transportation				
Morning After Brunch				
Total	$0.00	$0.00		$0.00

Quinceanera Planning Checklist

The following is meant to be fully inclusive. There are likely to be items that you do not need or want, or that are not in your budget for the event you are planning. If you are planning an event for hire, be sure to involve the family in making sure that any special family traditions for Quinceanera get handled. It is not uncommon for families to be so caught up in the celebration aspect of this event, that they become distracted. No one wants to ruin this special time by finding out that a special piece of family history was not honored when it is too late.

1+ Year Before Quinceanera

- ○ Book the Church
- ○ Book the Venue
- ○ Consider options for Damas & Chambelanes of the Court
- ○ If applicable consider who your sponsors, madrinas and padrinos could be
- ○ Book Photographer or Videographer
- ○ If a special Priest or Minister is wanted involve that person early
- ○ Hire Event Planner if needed
- ○ Consider catering, DJ's and Entertainment
- ○ Begin to Formalize themes

9 – 12 Months Before Quinceanera

- Decide on final Damas & Chambelanes
- Decide on final Damas & Chabelanes suits and dresses
- Select invitations, and floral arrangements
- Determine any special traditions to be honored such as the changing of shoes or last doll (symbolizing the transition into adulthood).
- Block rooms for out of town guests at a desirable hotel
- Finalize themes
- Order favors (dolls, shoes, crowns)
- Decide and choreograph any special dances the court may want to do together
- Book any rental items such as chairs, tents, or tables
- Finalize guest list
- Order invitations
- Audition and Book DJ/Entertainment
- Interview Photographer (questions included below)

6-9 Months Before Quinceanera

- Make Hotel Package with addresses, phone numbers and details for out of town guests
- Confirm rentals if renting tents, tables, chairs, chair covers etc.,
- Get invitations completed and assembled.
- Make transportation arrangements as needed for guests with no cars, or elderly who cannot drive
- Submit photos for a video montage set to music to play at the party if desired
- Make Hair and makeup appointments
- Order cake or deserts if not provided by caterer
- Select Limousine or Car company and book if applicable
- Re-confirm all church arrangements

1-2 Months Before Quinceanera

- Mail the invitations
- Submit music preferences or special songs to DJ
- Dress alterations and Suit/Tux Fittings
- Quinceanera prepares her welcome/thank you speech
- Pay for flowers, photographers, and provide deposits as required
- Obtain Bible, Prayer Book, Cross, Rosary, Scepter and other items suiting your traditions
- Finalize song list
- Finalize seating arrangements
- Purchase gifts for members of Quinceanera's Court
- Formal Photo of Quinceanera in her dress for display at the event
- Buy or put together gifts received book for thank you letters and memories

2-4 Weeks Before the Quinceanera

- Confirm quest list for non-responders
- Confirm head counts with Venue and Caterer
- Finalize prayers, speeches, or toasts
- Finalize and re-confirm all details with bakers, photographer, florist, and pay deposits as required – provide special requests for family photos to be taken
- Dance rehearsals, and final dress fitting

1 Week Before the Quinceanera

- Confirm brunch arrangements if needed
- Confirm hair and makeup appointments
- Make final payments to vendors
- Finalize seating chart
- Have a rehearsal at the Synagogue or Temple

Day of the Quinceanera

○	8-10:30 am	Hair and Makeup
○	10:30-11 am	Get Dressed
○	12-1:30 pm	Mass Ceremony (Pictures at Church)
○	2:30-3:30pm	Pictures at Beach, Park, Special places
○	4:00pm	Guests start arriving
○	4:30pm	Grand Entrance
○	4:30-5pm	Toasts from parents, padrinos etc.
○	5-7:00pm	Welcome from Quinceanera/Dinner
○	7-7:30pm	Change of Shoes & Last Doll
○	7:30-7:45pm	Father Daughter Dance
○	8:00-8:30pm	Quince Waltz or Surprise Dance
○	8:30-9:00pm	Cake Cutting/Serving
○	9:00-12:00	Party Down!

Venue Checklist

This checklist is to be used for interviewing venues, and tracking their answers to insure that they are a good fit for your or the client's needs. It is always a good idea to tour the venue early where economics permit, to see for yourself if the place is as nice as the well situated online pictures make it appear to be. When a venue impresses you, be sure to document that, and keep it mind. Relationships with quality reliable vendors are absolutely essential to success in this business.

Capacity

    _____ Invited Guest Capacity
    _____ Reception Area
    _____ Theatre/Meeting Room
    _____ Dining Area
    _____ Parking Capacity

Caterer

    _____ Exclusive caterers?
    _____ In-house tables/linens/chairs? If so, check out the quality.
    _____ Typical menu cost per head for cocktails, heavy appetizers, etc.
    _____ Bar tender charges?
    _____ Serving Charges?
    _____ Cake cutting charges?
    _____ Minimum food and beverage spend?
    _____ How early can your caterer arrive day of event to set up?

Rental Fees

- _____ Usually negotiable, especially for a major brand/off day
- _____ Does fee include a set up day?
- _____ How early/late can your teams load in?
- _____ Any discount for payment by check or early payment?
- _____ Hotels should waive any room rentals when F&B meets a min.

Bathrooms

- _____ Will you need to provide extra amenities to make the room nicer
- _____ Cleanliness – poorly kept restrooms reflect poorly managed venue
- _____ Number of stalls vs. number of guests

Parking

- _____ Existent?
- _____ Fee to use parking lot?
- _____ Valets – included? Is there a preferred valet company?
- _____ Buses – if using buses - is there room to turn around, unload?

Shipments

_____ Will the venue accept and store boxes a few days before event? $?

Audiovisual Team

_____ Exclusive AV Company?
_____ What tech operators are included, if any? (lighting tech, sound,   camera)
_____ Cost of in-house AV Team/hour/operator
_____ What AV exists in house? See the quality of the projector and check compatibility.
_____ Internet Access- speed and logistics (do you need to drop lines, $$$)
_____ Cost to use existing Internet lines

Stages

_____ Note any restrictions and size dimensions
_____ Height from ground to hang points
_____ See stage lighting with the room dark
_____ Existing backdrops, can you utilize these for event?
_____ If a stage must be brought in understand load-in logistics/restrictions

Registration/Place card area

_____ Is there a clean, open space near entrance of venue and in front of main room?

_____ How much signage can be placed outside of meeting room, in common areas?

_____ Will other events be held during the event?

_____ Does venue have staff to help with registration/guiding guests to room?

Entrance

_____ Opportunity to brand/decorate entrance area?

_____ Curb appeal; are you comfortable with the current look/feel of the entrance?

Reception Area

_____ How close is the area to the ceremony/meeting room?

_____ Ideally a large open space with the ability to brand/decorate

_____ What furniture can be utilized for event?

_____ Will venue take away existing furniture you don't want for your event?

Any charges?

_____ How early can you set up in this area?

Other Clients

_____ Who else has held events at this venue in
recent months?
_____ Testimonials? Can you contact references?
_____ Has a major competitor hosted parties at this
venue for a similar client base?

Electronic versions of this tool with room for notes are
available upon request at **products@newbizplaybook.com**.

Food and Beverage Planning

Appetizers

As you determine the appetizer quantity, consider what purpose the appetizers will serve. If you're serving appetizers before a main meal, you don't need as many as you do if the appetizers are the meal itself. Because appetizers are different from other food items, how much you need depends on several factors. Appetizers don't lend themselves to a quantity chart, per se, but let the following list guide you:

- For appetizers preceding a full meal, you should have at least four different types of appetizers and six to eight pieces (total) per person. For example, say you have 20 guests. In that case, you'd need at least 120 total appetizer pieces.

- For appetizers without a meal, you should have at least six different types of appetizers. You should also have 12 to 15 pieces (total) per person. For example, if you have 20 guests, you need at least 240 total appetizer pieces. This estimate is for a three-hour party. Longer parties require more appetizers.

- The more variety you have, the smaller portion size each type of appetizer will need to have. Therefore, you don't need to make as much of any one particular appetizer.

- When you serve appetizers to a crowd, always include bulk-type appetizers. Bulk-type foods are items that aren't individually made, such as dips or spreads. If you forgo the dips and spreads, you'll end up making hundreds of individual appetizer items, which may push you over the edge. To calculate bulk items, assume 1 ounce equals 1 piece.

- Always try to have extra items, such as black and green olives and nuts, for extra filler.

When appetizers precede the meal, you should serve dinner within an hour. If more than an hour will pass before the meal, then you need to increase the number of appetizers. Once again, always err on the side of having too much rather than too little.

Quantity planning for soups, sides, main courses, and desserts

The following tables can help you determine how much food you need for some typical soups, sides, main courses, and desserts. If the item you're serving isn't listed here, you can probably find an item in the same food group to guide you.

You may notice a bit of a discrepancy between the serving per person and the crowd servings. The per-person serving is based on a plated affair (where someone else has placed the food on the plates and the plates are served to the guests). In contrast, buffet-style affairs typically figure at a lower serving per person because buffets typically feature more side dish items than a plated meal does. Don't use the quantity tables as an exact science; use them to guide you and help you make decisions for your particular crowd. If you're serving a dish that you know everyone loves, then make more than the table suggests. If you have a dish that isn't as popular, you can get by with less.

Soups and Stews

Soup or Stew	Per Person	Crowd of 25	Crowd of 50
Served as a first course	1 cup	5 quarts	2-1/2 gallons
Served as an entree	1-1/2 to 2 cups	2 to 2-1/2 gallons	4 gallons

Menudo and Caldo doe Res are popular choices and can be done inexpensively

Main Courses

Entree	Per Person	Crowd of 25	Crowd of 50
Baby-back ribs, pork spareribs, beef short ribs	1 pound	25 pounds	50 pounds
Casserole/Enchiladas	N/A	Two or three 9-x-13-inch casseroles	Four or five 9-x-13-inch casseroles
Chicken, turkey, or duck (boneless)	1/2 pound	13 pounds	25 pounds
Chicken or turkey (with bones)	3/4 to 1 pound	19 pounds	38 pounds
Chili, stew, stroganoff, and other chopped meats	5 to 6 ounces	8 pounds	15 pounds

Ground beef	1/2 pound	13 pounds	25 pounds
Maine lobster (about 2 lbs. each)	1	25	50
Oysters, clams, and mussels (medium to large)	6 to 10 pieces	100 to 160 pieces	200 to 260 pieces
Pasta	4 to 5 ounces	7 pounds	16 pounds
Pork	14 ounces	22 pounds	44 pounds
Roast (with bone)	14 to 16 ounces	22 to 25 pounds	47 to 50 pounds
Roast cuts (boneless)	1/2 pound	13 pounds	25 pounds
Shrimp (large: 16 to 20 per pound)	5 to 7 shrimp	7 pounds	14 pounds
Steak cuts (T-bone, porterhouse, rib-eye)	16 to 24 ounces	16 to 24 ounces per person	16 to 24 ounces per person
Turkey (whole)	1 pound	25 pounds	50 pounds

Side Dishes

Side Dish	Per Person	Crowd of 25	Crowd of 50
Asparagus, carrots, cauliflower, broccoli, green beans, corn kernels, peas, black-eyed peas, and so on	3 to 4 ounces	4 pounds	8 pounds
Corn on the cob (broken in halves when serving buffet-style)	1 ear	20 ears	45 ears
Pasta (cooked)	2 to 3 ounces	3-1/2 pounds	7 pounds
Beans Potatoes and yams	1 (medium)	6 pounds	12 pounds
Rice and grains (cooked)	1-1/2 ounces	2-1/2 pounds	5 pounds

Side Salads

Ingredient	Per Person	Crowd of 25	Crowd of 50
Croutons (medium size)	N/A	2 cups	4 cups
Dressing (served on the side)	N/A	4 cups	8 cups
Fruit salad	N/A	3 quarts	6 quarts
Lettuce (iceberg	N/A	4 heads	8 heads

or romaine)

Lettuce (butter or red leaf)	N/A	6 heads	12 heads
Potato or macaroni salad	N/A	8 pounds	16 pounds
Shredded cabbage for coleslaw	N/A	6 to 8 cups (about 1 large head of cabbage)	12 to 16 cups (about 2 large heads of cabbage)
Vegetables (such as tomato and cucumber)	N/A	3 cups	6 cups

Breads

Bread	Per Person	Crowd of 25	Crowd of 50
Croissants or muffins	1-1/2 per person	3-1/2 dozen	7 dozen
Dinner rolls	1-1/2 per person	3-1/2 dozen	7 dozen
French or Italian bread	N/A	Two 18-inch loaves	Four 18-inch loaves

Desserts

Dessert	Per Person	Crowd of 25	Crowd of 50
Brownies or bars	1 to 2 per person	2-1/2 to 3 dozen	5-1/2 to 6 dozen
Cheesecake	2-inch wedge	Two 9-inch cheesecakes	Four 9-inch cheesecakes
Cobbler	1 cup	Two 9-x-9-x-2-inch pans	Four 9-x-9-x-2-inch pans
Cookies	2 to 3	3 to 4 dozen	6 to 8 dozen
Ice cream or sorbet	8 ounces	1 gallon	2 gallons
Layered cake or angel food cake	1 slice	Two 8-inch cakes	Four 8-inch cakes
Pie	3-inch wedge	Two or three 9-inch pies	Four or five 9-inch pies
Pudding, trifles, custards, and the like	1 cup	1 gallon	2 gallons
Sheet cake	2-x-2-inch piece	1/4 sheet cake	1/2 sheet cake

Alcohol and Beverage Planning

It is your choice as to whether to allow alcohol to be served at your event, but you will want to make sure that your venue has a license, or arrangements in place to allow you to serve, should you decide to do so.

Concerning drinks, let the following list guide you:

> Soft drinks: One to two 8-ounce servings per person per hour.

> Punch: One to two 4-ounce servings per person per hour.

> Tea: One to two 8-ounce servings per person per hour.

> Coffee: One to two 4-ounce servings per person per hour.

> Water: Always provide it. Two standard serving pitchers per table are usually enough.

> Again, err on the side of having too much. If people are eating a lot and having fun, they tend to consume more liquid.

Alcohol Consumption and Pricing Projection Tool

There is always some subjectivity in alcohol planning. The assumption here is that 75% of the guests are drinking alcohol. This should be discussed, as a higher percentage of children in attendance, a group of heavier drinkers etc., could impact these assumptions.

As always we recommend adding 10% to all estimates. You will frustrate guests if there is insufficient alcohol, so make sure they are in agreement with your assumptions on numbers. They will know their guests better than anyone. The cost estimates assume average costs on beer, wine, and liquor. Premium beer, wine, and liquor would also mean increased costs. This also assumes equal consumption i.e. 25% each of beer, wine, and liquor. Beer drinkers tend to range closer to 40%, but these figures make scaling for your needs much easier.

The following should help plan for reception alcohol consumption. BD = beer drinker, WD = wine drinker, LD = liquor drinker

	Small Wedding (100 guests)	
	Amount	Cost
Beer	5 cases per 25 BD	75.00
Wine	20 bottles per 25 WD	160.00
Liquor	6 750 ml bottles per 25 LD	90.00

	Medium Wedding (200 guests)	
	Amount	Cost
Beer	9 cases per 50 BD	135.00
Wine	40 bottles per 50 WD	320.00
Liquor	12 750 ml bottles per 50 LD	180.00

	Large Wedding (100)	
	Amount	Cost
Beer	3 Kegs 100 BD	270.00
Wine	79 bottles per 100 WD	632.00
Liquor	24 750 ml bottles per 100 LD	360.00

Seating Planning Tool

Banquet Table

Table Size	Seating Capacity	Linen Size	Space Needed
6'	6-8	90" x 132"	11" x 7"
8'	8-10	90" x 156"	13' x 7'
Classroom 6'	4	70" x 170"	11' x 6'
Classroom 8'	6	70" x 170"	13' x 6'

Round Table

Table Size	Seating Capacity	Linen Size	Space Needed
2.5'	2-4	96" round	7' diameter
3'	4-5	96" round	8' diameter
4'	6-8	108" round	9' diameter
5'	8-10	120" round	10' diameter
6'	10-12	132" round	11' diameter

Cocktail Table

Table Size	Seating Capacity	Linen Size	Space Needed
2.5'	2-4	108" round	7' diameter
3'	4-5	120" round	8' diameter

Dance Floor Planning Tool

This tool has been designed to allow you to plan and scale necessary floor space for dancing. For parties greater than 250, simply use multiples of the tables below. If more than 50% of guests are expected to be dancing, ignore the guests invited column, and plan based upon the number of dancers in the second column.

Total Guests	Dancers	Dance FL Size	Floor SQ Feet
24	12	8′x8′	64
36	18	8′x12′	96
48	24	8′x16′	128
64	32	12′x12′	144
72	36	12′x16′	192
90	45	12′x20	240
96	48	16′x16′	256
120	60	16′x24′	384
128	64	16′x24′	384
144	72	16′x24′	384
150	75	20′x20′	400
168	84	16′x28′	448
180	90	20′x24′	480
192	96	16′x32′	512
210	105	20′x28′	560
250	125	24′x28′	672

Guest List Management Tool

This tool is most easily used in spreadsheet form. An excel file tool is available at newbizplaybook.com. For those who want to download it.

With proper planning, a fair amount of information is needed on each guest including:

1. First and last name

2. Telephone number

3. Address and/or email address

4. Invitation sent

5. Confirmed for attending/or not

6. Confirmed for attending brunch, or pre-event dinner/or not – out of town guests for example

7. Quinceanera gift

8. Thank you letter sent

Download a great tool for helping the Quinceanera and parents keep track of attendance, and their responsibilities for thank you cards etc. This tool also helps the event planner to track and make adjustments for food, dance etc., in the event that more or fewer guests attend than expected. Electronic versions of this spreadsheet will be sent to readers upon request at **products@newbizplaybook.com**.

Vendor Contact Planning Sheet

Vendor	Business Name	Contact Name	Contact Number	Payment Status
Photographer				
Priest Minister				
Bakery				
Bar Tenders				
Wait staff				
Caterer				
Videographer				
D.J.				
Flowers				

Vendor Commitment Sheet

Vendor	Commitment	Arrival Time	Notes -	Gets Meal -
Photographer	8 hours x2			
Priest/Minister				
Bakery		2.pm		
Bar Tenders				
Wait staff				No
Caterer				
Videographer				
D.J.				
Flowers				

Invoice Template

Your invoice is as much a reflection of your brand as any business card. You want to finish your engagement as professionally as you started it. We have included a template, and an electronic copy is available at **products@newbizplaybook.com**. Your invoice should include all of the following:

[Company Name]
[Company slogan]

INVOICE

[Street Address]
[City, ST ZIP Code]
Phone [Phone] | Fax [Fax]
[Email] | [Website]

INVOICE # [Invoice No.]
DATE [Date]

TO
[Name]
[Company Name]
[Street Address]
[City, ST ZIP Code]
Phone [Phone] | [Email]

FOR [Project or service description]
P.O. # [P.O. #]

Description	Amount

Total

Make all checks payable to [Company Name]
Payment is due within 30 days.
If you have any questions concerning this invoice, contact [Name] | [Phone] | [Email]

THANK YOU FOR YOUR BUSINESS!

Photographer Interview Questions

Attached are some questions to ask when interviewing photographers, but prior to that, you should speak to your client about what they want in terms of Bar/Bat Mitzvah photography both in the deliverable, and with the style of photographer and his interaction with guests at the party. The photographer should be willing to answer these questions and this interview will give you a sense of his or her business temperament. Eventually you will have a stable of talented vendors who can help you here based on your specific needs, and you may develop special requests that help you make the events you handle unique. *You should also be prepared to provide the photographer with any needed information such as divorced guests, who do not wish to be photographed together etc.

1. Do you have my date available?

2. Do you have an online portfolio that I, and/or my client can review to get a sense of your style, and how recent is the material on it?

3. How far in advance do I need to book with you?

4. How long have you been in business/How many Quinceaneras have you shot?

5. Are there references you can offer from prior clients or planners? Note: This is the important question in the interview. Do not hire someone who cannot provide you this information, and call at least a couple of the references to compare their answers to your photographer's responses to these questions.

6. How would you describe your photography style (e.g. traditional, photojournalistic, and creative)?

7. How would you describe your approach to interacting with guests, i.e. blending in, stirring the pot for creative photos, choreographing shots?

8. What type of equipment do you use?

9. Are you shooting in digital or film format or both?

10. Do you shoot in color and black & white?

11. Can I give you a list of specific shots we would like?

12. How will you (and your assistants) be dressed?

13. Is it okay if other people take photos while you're taking photos?

14. Have you ever shot at my venue? If not, would you be willing to visit in advance to plan?

15. What time will you arrive at the site and for how long will you shoot?

16. If my event lasts longer than expected, will you stay? Is there an additional charge?

17. Can you put together a slideshow of the Quinceanera with provided photos and/or a real time slide show for viewing at the reception?

18. What information do you need from me before the event day?

19. What is your rate, and how is ownership of the photos handled? Parents may want to own the photos to copy and use as they see fit, and this may impact price.

20. Are you the photographer who will shoot my event? If not, who will shoot it, and can I see their work? If so, who will be assisting you and how?

21. What are your travel charges/requirements if any?

22. Are you photographing other events on the same day as this event?

23. What type of album designs do you offer? Do you provide any assistance in creating an album?

24. Do you provide retouching, color adjustment or other corrective services?

25. How long after the event will I get the proofs? Will they be viewable online? On a CD?

26. What is the ordering process?

27. How long after I order my photos/album will I get them?

28. Will you give me the negatives or the digital images, and is there a fee for that?

29. When will I receive a written contract?

30. What is your refund/cancellation policy? Do you have someone who covers your events in case of emergency or equipment failure?

Florist Interview Questions

1. Do you have my date available?

2. Do you have an online portfolio that I, and/or my client can review to get a sense of your style, and how recent is the material on it?

3. How far in advance do I need to book with you?

4. How long have you been in business/How many Bar/Bat Mitzvah's have you handled?

5. Are there references you can offer from prior clients or planners? Note: This is the important question in the interview. Do not hire someone who cannot provide you this information, and call at least a couple of the references to compare their answers to your florists responses to these questions.

6. Given the size of this event, flower preference, color scheme, and venue specifics for Synagogue/Temple and reception, what would you propose?   Note: Do not lead with your budget. Advise that you are open and want to see the proposal for a few different packages, so that you can compare costs.

7. What time will you arrive at the site and how long will it take you to set up?

8. Who will be managing the setup?

9. Are you providing flowers for other events on the same day as this event?

10. Any rental fees for vases or decorations the florist is providing?

11. Any additional labor charges, taxes, or other fee?

12. When will I receive a written contract?

13. What is your refund/cancellation policy? Do you have someone who covers your events in case of emergency? Note: It is common to require a 50% down payment.

DJ Details

What style DJ do you want: Quiet (no interaction during dancing) Moderate (interaction only if necessary) Outgoing (lots of interaction)

Is it more important for you to hear your favorite music, or for your guests to be dancing? _____

How many crowd-involvement songs would you like played (Electric Slide, Duck Dance, Cha Cha Slide, Cupid Shuffle, Anniversary Dance, etc.)?

These questions asked of your client will help to frame the experience they can expect from their DJ.

Quinceanera Reception Planning Tool

Contact Information

Client name: Phone/Email:

Quinceanera name:

Reception Date: Setup Start Time:

Entertainment Start Time: End Time:

The following is a typical but optional sequence of events. The specifics should be coordinated with relevant venders such as caterers, and DJ's etc.

Sequence	Time	Event
		Caterer Arrives begins setup
		DJ Arrives sets up and begins to play
		Main Reception Starts (guests join each other in main hall)
		Family Entrance
		Grand Entrance
		Toast
		Dinner
		Change of Shoes and Last Doll
		Father Daughter Dance
		Quince Waltz/Surprise Dance
		Guest of Honor/Parent Dance
		Cake Cutting
		Open Dancing
		Finale

Venue Information

There are other tools in this publication for helping you to interview, plan for, and qualify the venue for your event. Those may be used here, so for example, there is a guest tracker in the wedding section. You may want to use something different for this event, but that will work here.

Name/address of establishment:

Contact name: Phone:

Primary room name/location:

Planning Logistics

Number of guests: Children:

Party Theme:

Number of courses to be served (including dessert):

Will the caterer be using the dance floor for a buffet during the cocktail hour?   During the main course?

Contact Information for Other Party Professionals

	Name	Phone	email	Booked From_ to _
Caterer	Grande Dining Cuisine	(123)456-789	abc@def.com	7-9:30
Banquet Hall/Venue				
Planner/Coordinator				
Photographer				
Videographer				
Entertainer				

Cocktail Hour Planning Tool

Is cocktail hour in same room as main reception?   If not, what room is it in?

Music for cocktail hour:
Reception Start (Guests enter main reception room from cocktail room)

Music to start with (high-energy dance music recommended):

Reception Grand Entrance / Introductions

Who will be performing the introductions?

Suggested order of introductions:

1.   Parents (usually introduced as Host and Hostess, Bob and Jane)

2.   Siblings

3.   Guest of Honor

Re songs requested, if not review DJ reference tool for a feel about requests on music options, and DJ style preferences.

Please list those to be introduced during the grand entrance in the order they will be introduced. You can choose different songs for each person or one for the entire group. Use additional sheets if necessary. If you want, interesting tidbits of information about relationships to the guest of honor can be announced—if so, please write details below each person's name.

For each name collect:

Name(s)

Phonetic Pronunciation(s)

How to Introduce

Music

Candle lighting

This is a special ceremony in which the Quinceanera takes time to honor those who have been important in her live, by selecting 15 people, including parents, siblings, other family, and close friends. During the ceremony she dedicates a candle to each of those she has chosen, and as she lights each, the DJ plays a special song. When all candles are lit, she delivers them to those in attendance, while telling the guests why this person is so special in her life. For special people who have passed, the Quinceanera leaves their candles in place, lit as a reminder that these special folks are still with her, and she celebrates their impact in her life with those in attendance.

Include the names of people who will be involved

1. Grandparents
2. Aunts
3. Uncles
4. Cousins
5. Older relatives
6. Younger relatives
7. Friends of parents
9. Siblings
10. Guests of Honor
11. Parents

Symbolic Gifts

Many families choose the moment of her Quinceanera to celebrate a daughter's coming of age with special gifts. Common gifts include:

1. Bible
2. Rosary
3. Cross or Medal
4. 15 Roses
5. Tiara and Scepter
6. Special family jewelry or heirlooms

Changing of the Shoes and The Last Doll

A common tradition shared with a father and daughter, or if the father has passed or is not around, a grandfather, or older brother.

The Quinceanera is seated, and the father removes her shoes, changing them for different, more mature shoes. A doll is also offered to the girl, her last doll, in recognition of her transition to adulthood. Some families have ribbons pinned to the doll that the Quinceanera shares with her quests, as a way of insuring that she has thanked all in attendance. In some families, the Quinceanera presents that doll to a younger sibling as a special gift.

Celebrating Sponsors and Guests of Honor

It is very common in latin cultures for parents to pay for part of the Quinceanera celebration, and to have help from friends and family, often called sponsors.

This is a highly respected role in the celebration, and time is often taken to thank these sponsors, where the Quinceanera publicly shows her gratitude, and recognizes them for the honors they have bestowed upon her.

This is done at different times, and is handled in the traditional manner of a toast.

Candle Lighting List

Name(s)	Phonetic Pronunciation(s)	How to Introduce	Music
1.			
2.			
3.			
4.			
5.			
6.			

Grand Finale

Before the last dance, we can organize guests into a circle around the guest of honor, pass the mic around, and allow them to each offer best wishes. Do you want to do this?

Table Photos/Interviews

Please indicate the points (if any) during the reception when you and your photographer want everyone to remain seated for table photos:

Please indicate the points (if any) during the reception when you and your videographer want everyone to remain seated for table interviews:

If the photographer or videographer requests it, do you want us to clear the dance floor or delay the start of dancing for the completion of table photos and/or interviews?

Additional setups require:
Dedications, Birthdays, Anniversaries, Other Special Dances, etc.
List any special announcements you would like us to make. This is a great way to personalize your event and recognize someone special.

Additional Notes *(Use back or additional sheets if necessary)*
If there is anything else we need to know to ensure your reception flows smoothly, please list the details here. In particular:

- If you feel we need to be aware of Any sensitive information regarding your event, family, or guests
- If you are having a video presentation, a singer, musicians, fraternity/sorority serenade, centerpiece giveaway, or any other personalized additions that will make your party unique

Quinceanera Theme Ideas

1. Hollywood
2. Fairytale (with colors chosen from famous stories)
3. Mardi Gras
4. Candy land (used for decorations and to add color that fits the pallet chosen by the quinceanera)
5. Masquerade
6. Renaissance
7. Carnival
8. Under the Sea
9. Dios De Los Muertos
10. Traditional Western
11. Fiesta
12. Bohemian
13. Great Gatsby Roaring 20's
14. Charro
15. Enchanted Forest/Evening
16. Winter Wonderland
17. Beauty and the Beast
18. A Night in Paris
19. Flamenco
20. Black and White Ball

Quinceanera Invitation Template

Mr. Martin Montenegro & Mrs. Maria Montenegro

-Are pleased to invite you -

*To the Celebration of The Fifteenth
Birthday of Their Daughter*

Celeste Montenegro

*The holy mass in her honor will take place:
Saturday August 18th, 2017 at 11:00 a.m.
Saint Helen's Catholic Church
1010 Buck Street, Houston, TX*

*Please RSVP by 5/5/17 to Rosa Garcia at
222-222-2222 or rosa@madeupemail.com*

*Chamberlain of Honor
Jose Rodriguez*

Damas	*Chamberlains*
Stephanie Smith	*Jesus Rebenga*
Giselle Sanchez	*Alex Rodriquez*
Laura Avalos	*Jorge Avalos*
Ashley Montalvo	*Luis Cisneros*

Made in the USA
Monee, IL
26 April 2021